S0-CIF-029

Miró Mirror

Miró Mirror

poems

Robley Whitson

WITHDRAWN
NDSU

books
1995

Miró Mirror
by
Robley Whitson

Library of Congress Catalog Card Number

95-070031

International Standard Book Number

1-55605-260-X

Copyright ©1995 by Robley Whitson

ALL RIGHTS RESERVED

QH Books
Cloverdale Corporation
Bristol, IN46507-9460

PS
3573
· H554
M5
1995

Printed in the United States of America

for
Deborah

MIRÓ MIRROR

Paintings

    For Joan Miró the initial moment of creative vision is always the unexpected surfacing of something extraordinary from his unconscious into consciousness. In an idle moment of sketching suddenly there it is, taking recognizable form. From that point on creation is hours and days of intense labor to translate vision into line, shape, color.

    The complexes of multidimensional symbols whereby the unconscious speaks within dream or a drawing hand are transformed into the simplest possible elements. They are then framed together in compositions designed to defy the sense of the static imposed by the two-dimensional rectangle of the canvas.

    Miró's commitment is to a surreal vision of reality— the most elusive reality of the silent deep of mind as made visible in the seemingly controlled reality of concrete things to see.

    The real and the surreal: the meeting of two kinds of consciousness with two languages speaking at once. We can recognize the shapes— eyes, stars, ladders, bodies— but we realize we are seeing something more and something else, often disturbingly *other* than what we expected.

    Miró always identifies the central moment of each of these complex experiences with a concrete title, some by a simple element (*Bather; The Wind*), others by phantasmic symbols (*The Bird with a Calm Look, its Wings in Flames; Hair Disheveled by the Fleeing Constellations*).

The initial moment of these poems also surfaced unexpectedly, sparked by Miró's titles and the visions inside his pictures— by the ways of seeing provoked by them. Some of the poems reflect directly the elements of the picture (such as *Horse at Seashore*). But most of the poems fly away, into their own further visions of the central moment (such as *Ciphers & Constellations in Love with a Woman*).

All of the poems may be thought of as parallax seeings of Miró seeing— something like the shift in sight that occurs when we see an object through a second medium (the stick in water that seems to break in two: an air-stick that ends at the water surface and a disjoined water-stick that begins under the surface).

In effect a surreal vision allows for (calls for?) as many visions as there are visionaries— as many parallaxes as there are vantage points for sightings. The poems are mirrors, but surreal mirrors: they do not *represent again,* they *present another*.

The images accompanying the poems are drawn from elements in the original Miró paintings, but adapted not reproduced— paraphrases not quotations. Apart from *hommage à Miró*, these, like his titles, touch the initial moment of vision.

Parallax poems and parallax images, surreal mirrors which, hopefully, do much more than reflect. Odd mirrors for hearing as well as seeing that which is ultimately always ineffable and invisible but which, nonetheless, keeps coming up to disturb the surface, our surface.

The Wind

If you knew me
it would have to be
from inside the wind,
the wind that blows away
the mystery of the moon
with the skittering of leaves
old and dry and forgotten.

To live in such a wind
is to live in a tower,
in its high fastness
where I can dream
everything in glass,
everything seen into its center
all the surfaces open
inviting me to look
long and unembarrassed.

It is a wind of secrets—
the secret in wheels
turning on unmoving hub holes
running away on rims
unable to rest anywhere,
the wheels of dust
revolving into starlight
and masses of stars
cartwheeling everywhere still empty.

This wind catches up
silent passengers,
silent because so surprised
at being whirled away
sometimes even all over any place,
when they always thought
they would stay home
and die there, as usual.

3

All the flying passengers
dream everything in glass
just as I do
so we are all transparent,
wide open to each other.
Even though there are surfaces
we pay no attention
as we stare at the centers
where the mystery of the moon
is blown round and round.

I keep looking at it
—we all do—
but it will not stay still.
I am just about to see,
but that moon circles
into some other someone-center

—like looking at the light
and seeing those little floaters
that swim inside eyes,
always getting in the way
yet always slipping aside
when I try to look
right at them—

but are they in my eye
or far out there
or somewhere in between?—
little floater centers everywhere,
masses of eye stars
cartwheeling anywhere
inside the wind

where I am,
if you knew me.

The Birth of the World

Splotched dots
in flight from black angles,
everything in streaks—
       the way it really was
       ideally always is.

Energy does it:
       keeps dots from being
       all around truly round—
       keeps angles black
       the color points must be—
       keeps everything in streaks
       faster than light
so the world can get born.

The Song of the Vowels

The sounds of air
clear and simple,
columned through a throat,
shaped within a mouth
by unclosed lips—
sound left undefined
not formed to words,
the sound of song
breathed open mouthed.

A vowel song says nothing,
just wanders on—
mindless moments of flow
eyes in blank focus
until melody trails off, over.

After a pause:
Sigh.
Then...things again.

Letters and Numbers Attracted by a Spark

Letters and numbers,
bugs swarming a light
into words and sums
that say and solve everything—
maybe, for a moment—
then a scramble mumble
of brain sparks.

The vowel of zero:
0
round as a mouth,
the circle sound
a surround of things—
or, the enclosing naught,
a nothing, gone off somewhere.

That pointless vowel:
A
a something or a someone,
so indefinite.

Ah, but other vowels:
I
I, the one Me
U
You too...with Me
Then E
We
Yes, oh Yes!

People at Night, Guided by
the Phosphorescent Tracks of Snails

Slug slime,
phosphorescence
light-bearing essence
gleaming in moonlight:
meanderinqs
mindless lines
looped, crossed, retraced—

Memory from oceans ago
draws us two by two,
and we follow the tracks
into the glow
we still dream of—
before we learned to breathe,
when our lidless eyes
could see everything.

Horse at Seashore

Sometimes there is a red sky,
not just sunset red—
a red fever fire
in a shore-racing horse.

Somehow he has swallowed
the real sky, the blue one,
with the whole tan land
and the nearly black sea—
all of them now a new world
inside his white body.

So the left-behind-world
is smudging darker darker,
sand dunes are mountains,
and that red sky horizon
flows into waves
without any water.

A strange horse—
but not to the horse:
a strange world inside.

The Nightingale's Song at Midnight and Morning Rain

The darkest part of night
earth turned, this spot
farthest around from the sun,
and we lie here, quiet
not wanting to speak words
not even hearing our breaths,
fearing our pulses might
break the silence
we so need right now.

At this midnight mid-now
a nightingale sings—
an absolute sound:
song of a bird for a bird.
Not for us, ignored
as if we were somewhere else
not here in their world.

Of course we are somewhere else—
We will wake up there
in the morning
in the rain
in its hitting noise.

Awakening in the Early Morning

Sunset and moonrise
eyes close.
Sunrise and moonset
eyes open.
A seamless cycle

but not of infinite circles:
off-center ellipses
where dreams end too soon
right in the middle of
something—

would have been wonderful,
whatever it was
No! still is,
somewhere around the curve
in another dream.

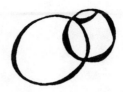

Sunrise

Dawn and light,
everything visible again—
people and birds,
all the near-infinity of stuff
that gets in the way—

Everything seen but stars,
there only in the dark
all of them with us
as if we alone are alone—

Then the sun comes,
and delusions of daytime.
We can make them go away
if we close our eyes,
but there are no stars inside.

The Red Sun Gnaws at the Spider

Hot day coming—
red sun says so,
red sun always knows.

Red sun also gnaws
at all the dots of dew
whorled on the threads
of the spider web—
trying to get the spider.

But she sees him
with all her nine eyes,
tiny black pin-point eyes
set for every direction—
No sun, red or whatever,
gets a bite of her.

Not with eight legs
ready to zip up silk
and into her lair
to wait for sunset
when she knows he has to go.

Then back to spinning,
and the killing.

Personages in Front of a Volcano

Volcanic confrontation—
soft dry people
facing lava rivers,
crust cool and cooling
center molten still.
Thousand mile sheets,
layered folded rock,
squeezing by each other
adrift on magma sea.

Two or three or so
of our billions
roam those stone slabs
afloat above the oceans.

Hot ash in the air,
but people are there
as in a wind making clouds
to rain someplace into mud
into seeds and trees
for people who split open
into volcanoes.

The Farmers' Meal

The farmer husband—

> Forests of animals
> bushes and weeds
> all at peace.

The farmer wife—

> Now no more hunters,
> no women and children
> pulling roots and stripping twigs.

At their noontime table—

> Now chickens and cows
> sheep, pigs and all the rest
> bred and fed, cared for.

Surprise! food for us,
piece by piece—
None for you!

Traitor dogs must dance for scraps.

Dog Barking at the Moon

Wolf! Wolf!

I am! I am!
Barking up the moon,
grown rounder and rounder
till night is white.

If I were a wolf,
really,
I would howl,
really,
call all the wolves
to climb up
into the moon,
into its volcanoes,
fill them with
full moon fools.

If I were a werewolf—
feel a growl
rising louder louder

Wolf! Wolf!

Frighten you—
like ant ropes
winding up the table legs
to the honey pot
you left open—

Frighten you—
like your aunt's throat
clutched by pearls
three or four strands
to cover her turkey neck—

Frighten you—
like my slant gropes
in the dark room,
should be love forever
except for the unlikely
stray silver bullet.

When I was a wolfman,
really,
there were no bullets yet—
just knives and arrows
of mere iron and steel,
scarcely any silver ones.
So we howled and howled
our weird wolf songs
and you locked your doors
and looked at our moon
through cracks in the shutters,
scared.

Hair Disheveled by the Fleeing Constellations

Dot lights and dusts
a red Mars
a green slice of Moon
a grapefruit yellow Sun,
all in wild flight
from the black spider star
caught in the writhe
of her tangled hair.

They are terrified of it
and so of her—
These two together the new center
of everything rushing away.

A woman vowed to the spider
who webs her in silk—
She promised not to comb her hair.

Women Haunted by the Passage of
the Bird-Dragonfly, Omen of Bad News

News is always bad—
because it's new:
it's not what is,
what was till now.
All that is gone
flown into empty air.
It might dart and hover
as if to stay,
but she knows
the feel of
Gone
from the ghosts of eggs
inside her.

Women Encircled by the Flight of a Bird

Of all the things that fly
only birds —certain birds—
create circles,
great joined spiral arcs
flown round and round
some invisible center—
invisible to us, not them.

Still-point women:
where it always all begins,
inside them;
then outside them
where it will end.

The circling birds know this,
round and round
waiting.

Women at the Beach

They gather in sight of the sea
almost to the edge
to the high tide mark,
lie there in the glare,
skins against sand—
burning etched
into soft copper plates
to yield a single print
untitled
signed in pencil.

Women Resting

Resting
from being women,
from being human,
from being—

Resting
in being women, human—

That sharp line
where being shifts shape:

from
        becoming
in

where all the shapes shift
and everyone becomes golden,
whatever anyone was before—

that gold within eggs
suggesting light
but much faster,
so all are always there
before anything—

suggesting
rest.

**Women at the Border of a Lake
Irradiated by the Passage of a Swan**

Trees line the summer lake.
Shadow-leaves hover over water.
Women lean back into the cool,
feel the rough of bark
and prickle mat of weeds
mold their still soft skin
with tangled weave-marks.

Out in the sun a songless swan
parts the surface calm,
its long arrow ripple
flaring away from the white point
towards two shores—
one where the women wait
for the glitter of the wake
to flicker across their open bodies.

Never fooled by sweeps of breeze
spattering the glare in sparks,
they have been so long quiet
their woman-dark aware:
      everything is motionless;
      the silent swan is undulating light;
      ritual of shadows, done.

Bather

It is always
again,
even the first time,
because water is there first—
there before anyone,
there in us
our salt sea bodies.

Water within is unfelt.
Even the rolling tide of blood
would wait a million years
for us to find it.

But entering the water...

It is outside us—
we feel ripples and waves,
we feel ourselves lighten,
seem to flow
almost float apart,

almost—
if it were not for horizons
that draw the sharp line
between sky and sea,
the red sun and me—
both of us swimming
insideout.

The Rose Dusk Caresses
the Sex of Women and Birds

Turning to the sun
then with the sun
and now away,
the whole day of lights
from orange rising
to final rosing—

waiting for this last time
eyes can see to caress,
watching birds fly up
high enough to catch
the final red flash
under their feathers,
feeling the color from cloud lines
deepen into woman-dark—

a touch he will never understand:
he sees her only here,
not the disappearance,
the rosed birds
gone among the trees.

The Kiss

Kiss is a thin wind
wound around itself—
with a sound of someone,
someone who is
certain:
  circles never close,
  but loop open
  for a moment
  of tease.

Sunburst Wounds the Tardy Star

An open wound,
the skin pierced
poised on the edge
of the outside.
A wound inside
too deep to bleed,
surface showing no sign.
So no one knows.

Her soft fingertip
searches him for a scar.
He points to the place
though the skin is smooth—
she cannot feel to find it.

But he is pointing somewhere else,
through the place and beyond,
to the wound and beyond—
far off to some star
that leaves no mark
when it bursts apart
inside.

Her finger stops—

Look how late it is!

Flame in Space and Nude Woman

Empty space—
someone says
      redundant:
      space is empty.
I say
      empty, empty, empty
      infinitely empty
      infinite space—
      only space can never be
      redundant!

Something like a nude woman
      not naked,
      nude:
      simply herself
      nothing added
      nothing more needed,
      unneeding nude.

So, a flame,
not light—
light would fill the space,
be something on her skin
much more than cloth;
and after the light turned off
she would be left naked;
but after the flame died down
she would be nude,
just herself,
like space.

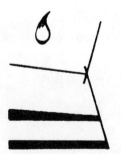

Ciphers & Constellations in Love with a Woman

She gazes into the shapes
her eyes play with stars—
the lions and bears
scorpions and crabs,
and all the people
even goddesses and gods.

She likes to sweep and linger
pause and dart off,
tease them with her glance.

Tantalizing eyes.

She knows they love her,
every one of them—
she must keep them eager,
not look long at any one,
not stop, trapped.

But the ciphers love her too,
those in-between-empty-spaces
the lightless zero voids,
the places with no shapes
nothing her eyes can catch.
She tries to skip past them,
see only star shapes
flirt with constellations—
flee the fearsome empty lover.

Empty—
Unimagined.

The Escape Ladder

Desperate,
nowhere left to stand—
The sky!
escape up, fly off
every direction open,
limitless spaces
between the stars.

Exhausted,
air the same everywhere—
The earth!
climb down, rest
here at last
one actual place
never to stir.

Or, stay on the ladder
on the mid-rung,
not go up
not come down—
free of all of them.

Personages with Star

All the stars,
or, one.
All the people,
or, one only,
alone—
perhaps lonely,
or not.

Stars burn away,
waste into cinder—
this one star
already dark,
invisible empty sky.

Black orbits,
blank people circling,
or bits of ash dust
falling into them—
small people
going round and round
growing smaller smaller.

All except one:
tall always taller—
        standing where?
        higher than what?—
tall beyond light years
until there is no measure.
So the stars stop.
Too lonely.

The Ladder Brushed the Firmament

Started climbing
so long ago now
I remember only spokes
and not looking down
or up,
hands on spokes
one always holding
one always reaching.

So long ago now
there is no up or down
and I can look anywhere
all over every direction,
out to the runaway stars
even to the inside firmament.
With no more up or down
I might try
stepping off the ladder.
I might.

Hand Catching a Bird

To catch a bird snatched
  out of blue sky—
a cloud hand
  of wavery wind fingers.

Unguessed gust:
  a bird blown
  dropped into a hand—
    just there,
    just happens to be.

Surprise!— bird
Surprise!— hand

Person Throwing a Stone at A Bird

Birds start as stones,
odd hard ovoids of various colors—
birds are the soft centers.

Thrown stones fly
an elegant arc,
once only
unless picked up again.

This one flies with a bird—
at a dart-off-bird
who flees the thrower,
a man on foot
unable to fly
unless he lets fly.

The Migratory Bird

Coming and going,
to and from
both at the same moment
        opposites together in us
every time we move—
there even in a return
to where we were from,
        where we think we were from
same places, same people
        never the same.

The space and time
we moved
        the void behind us,
        whatever ahead, pushed aside.

But those birds,
for millions of years—
        They only think they return,
even to the same tree
or the same rock ledge—
        All new feathers and twigs!

The Bird with Plumage Spread
Flies Toward the Silvery Tree

The wind this morning
warns of a storm
as it turns up
shimmering undersides of leaves
that rustle end-of-summer.
The invisible feel of breeze
moves a sight and a sound—
blown against the trees
and flown by a bird
on wing spread fingers
of impossible feathers
able to flow on air
among the silvery leaves.

The Passage of the Divine Bird

None can describe its flight,
though we think we know
what it cannot be
or should not be—
not dart or swoop,
no labored flapping.

Something elegant, majestic—
a great soaring arc perhaps,
or a raptor plummet
from the dazzle of the sun.
Possibly all of these;
just as possibly, none.

This is no bird bird
but a divine bird,
and it is more than flight:
it is passage,
passage through our lives
through each life.

That is how we know
this bird is divine—
as it passes through life,
mere life,
mine,
merely passes
never pauses, stops—
nor do I,
nor can I.

The Beautiful Bird Revealing
the Unknown to a Pair of Lovers

Lovers,
all the kinds
men, women, old, young—
as many kinds
as all of them,
two by two.

At that one moment,
the moment together,
they discover
the beautiful bird flying.

Later they wonder:
        Why did we look up?
and laugh into tears:
        How do we know
        the bird is beautiful?

The bird never asks itself:
        Why did I fly there then?
it never questions:
        How beautiful I am!
        Beautiful with them!

So the beautiful bird
unknows,
and flies with lovers.

For that one moment:
The Unknown.

The Bird with a Calm Look,
Its Wings in Flames

I fly the world
beyond everything and everyone,
through nights of stars
sleeping on the wind,
into days of sunfire
wings in flames.

Wherever I look
I see all of you
and all you do—
I see you kind and cruel,
I see you loving and killing.

You are puzzled, even angry:
      Come down!
      Bless the lovers,
      Stop the killers—

No!—you can do all that.
Come up!
And I will show you
how I do not burn
though I fly forever
my wings in flames.

Persons Attracted by the Form of a Mountain

To rise
every moment higher,

and every higher moment
to diminish,

apparently
diminish to a point—

at the point
disappear,

undimensional:

Mountainously
unhigh undeep unthick

Instantaneously—
to be that,

that.

Persons in the Presence of a Metamorphosis

Changes,
all sorts of changes—
and Change,
a real change,
one so different afterwards
only what used to be
before it happened
speaks in words.

We are always
—every single second—
there, here
at the transform moment when
then
escapes,
disappears different.

So we say
nothing,
not a sound.
Otherwise there would be
no change
and we would be left
this way,
as before.

Toward the Rainbow

Late summer afternoon.
East running rain.
Then the color comes.

Over rolling fields of grass
stretched as far as it goes,
a wet green smell.

At the cliff edge
with spray from below.

Any water lensing light.

Rainbows—
coming as storms stop,
fading away as we race
to reach where they touch down.

Rainbows—
even when we know
all about prisms
and eyes.

The Red Disk

The last moments before setting
the disk hangs round red
in the heat and haze of dust—
a sun we can watch
without the dazzle blind—
      what this star will look like
      at the long after end
      beyond the cindering burst
      that will purge the earth
      of anything like us—
a red disk ember sun
to die in circles of ashes,
about to go down tonight
in our eyes.

Personages and Birds Rejoicing
at the Arrival of the Night

Between all the days
there is always night,
a single great night
ready to emerge in shadows
after exhausted stars wander off.

The night was there
before any of them,
before anyone thought of light,
or imagined it good, but dark evil,
and sought to divide them
set the bright sparks free
so there would be night no more.

But the daystars blow apart,
wastes of deadened dust,
half-lives, half half-lives
half again and on
into no life at last—
then night at last, again.

The night of no-thing,
emptied of all the stuffing—
the pure awe always there
between undreamed days—

We begin in night:
People within mothers
birds within shells.
We take shape, grow
without delusions, then.
And when we finally awake
at day-end,
without delusion ever again.